MINDFUL MOMENTS

Relaxation Coloring Book for Adults

By Beauty in Books

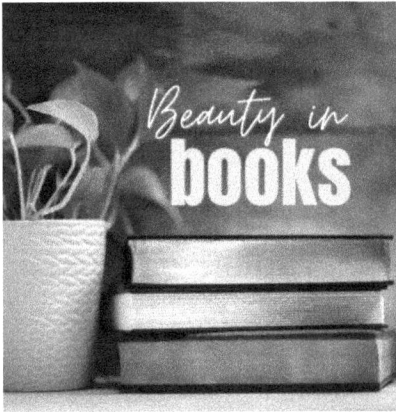

About the Author

"Aby Sparklewood is an accomplished author with a unique talent for crafting captivating children's fiction and insightful business books. With a playful imagination and a keen business sense, her stories ignite young minds and inspire entrepreneurs to reach new heights of success."

You are Stronger than your worries

Find Peace in this moment

You are stronger than you think.

Breathe Breathe in calm, exhale stress.

What doesn't break you makes you stronger

Calm mind Calm life

Your Peace is your Power

Find
Stillness in
the chaos

Trust the Timing of of your Life

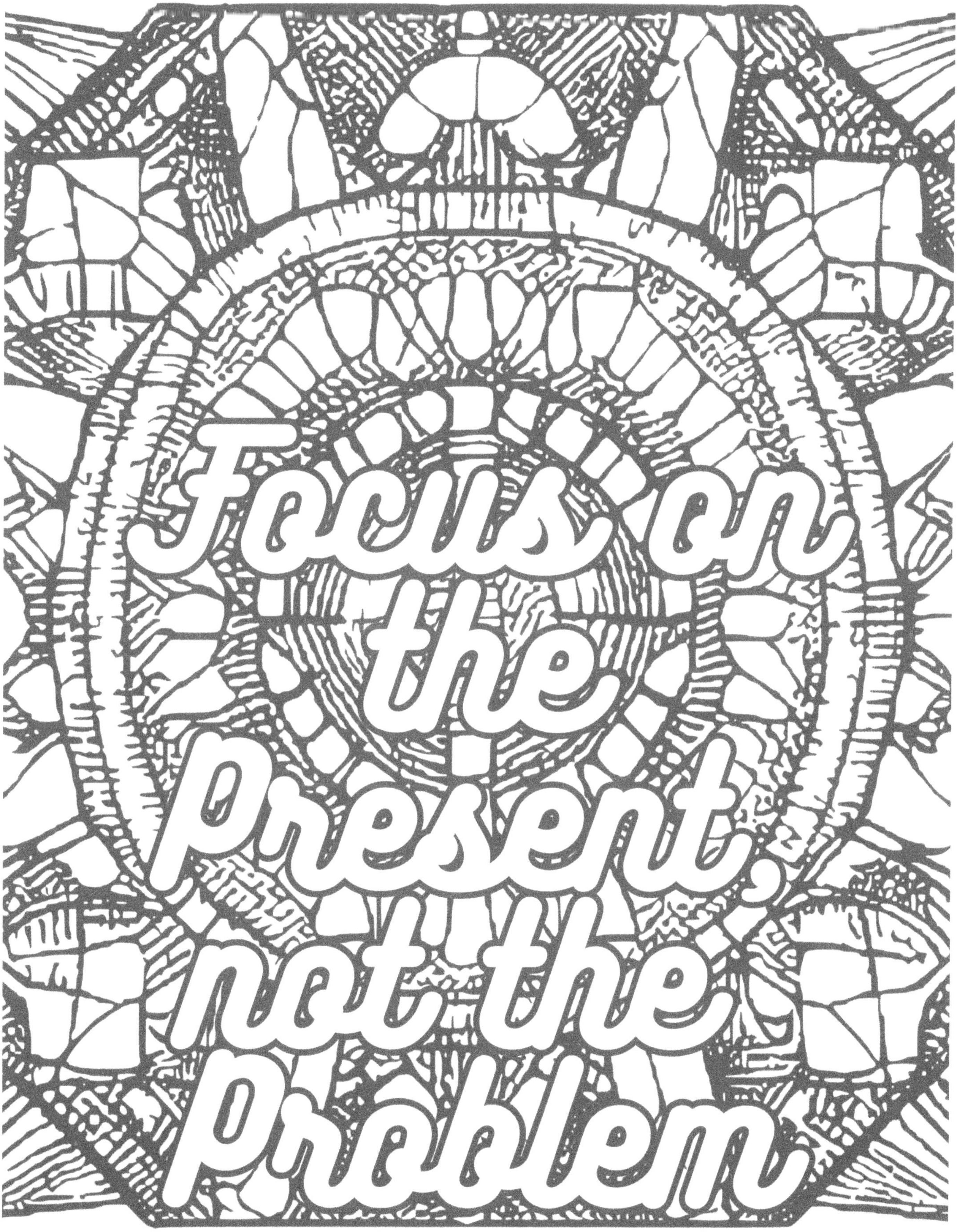
Focus on the Present, not the Problem

Stress spelled backward is desserts!

Stress is an illusion; peace is real

The sun will rise and so will you.

Chaos breeds creativity.

Stress is a teacher, learn from it

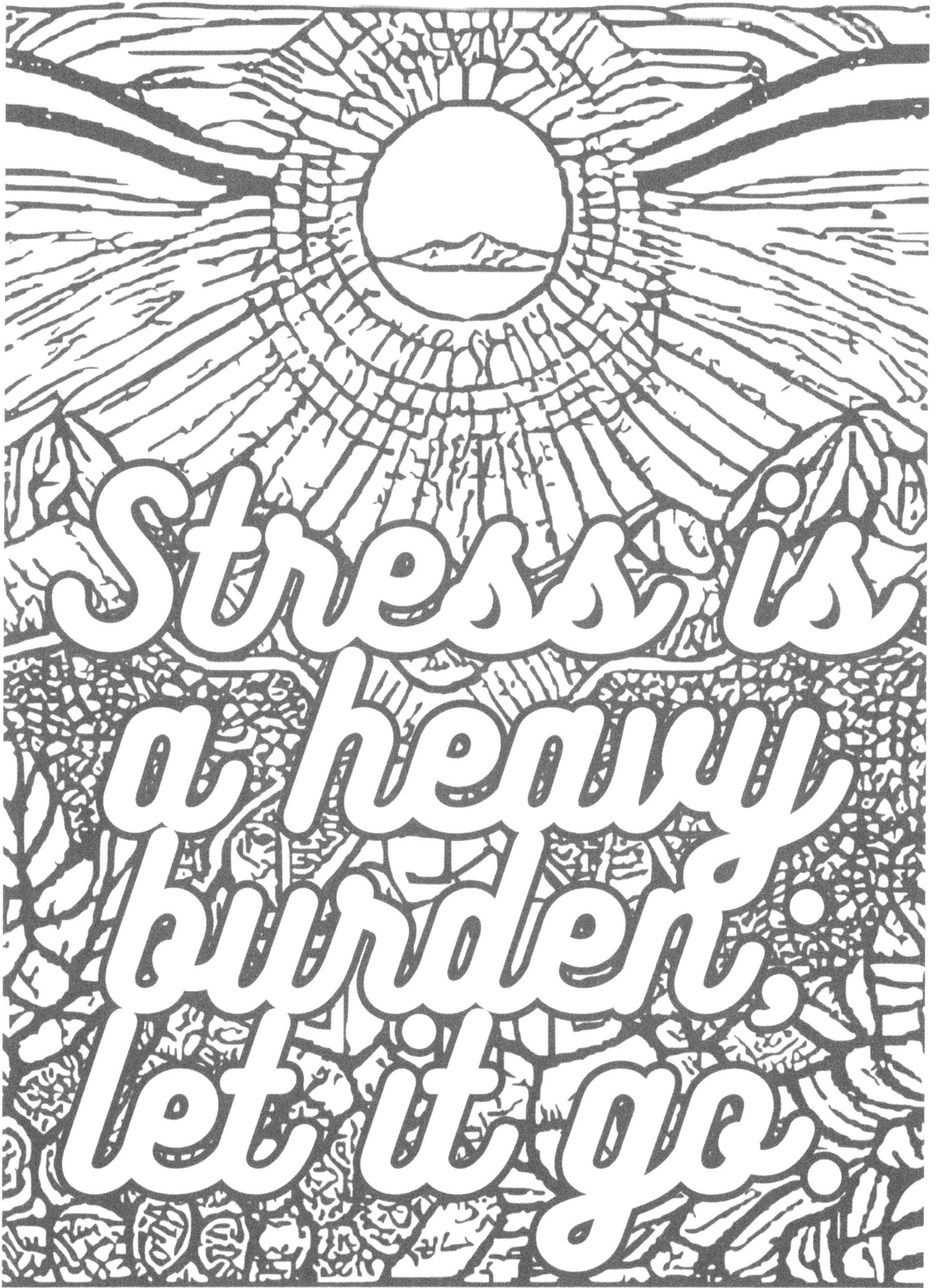

Stress is a heavy burden. let it go.

Let gratitude be your guide.

Breathe deeply and let go of tension.

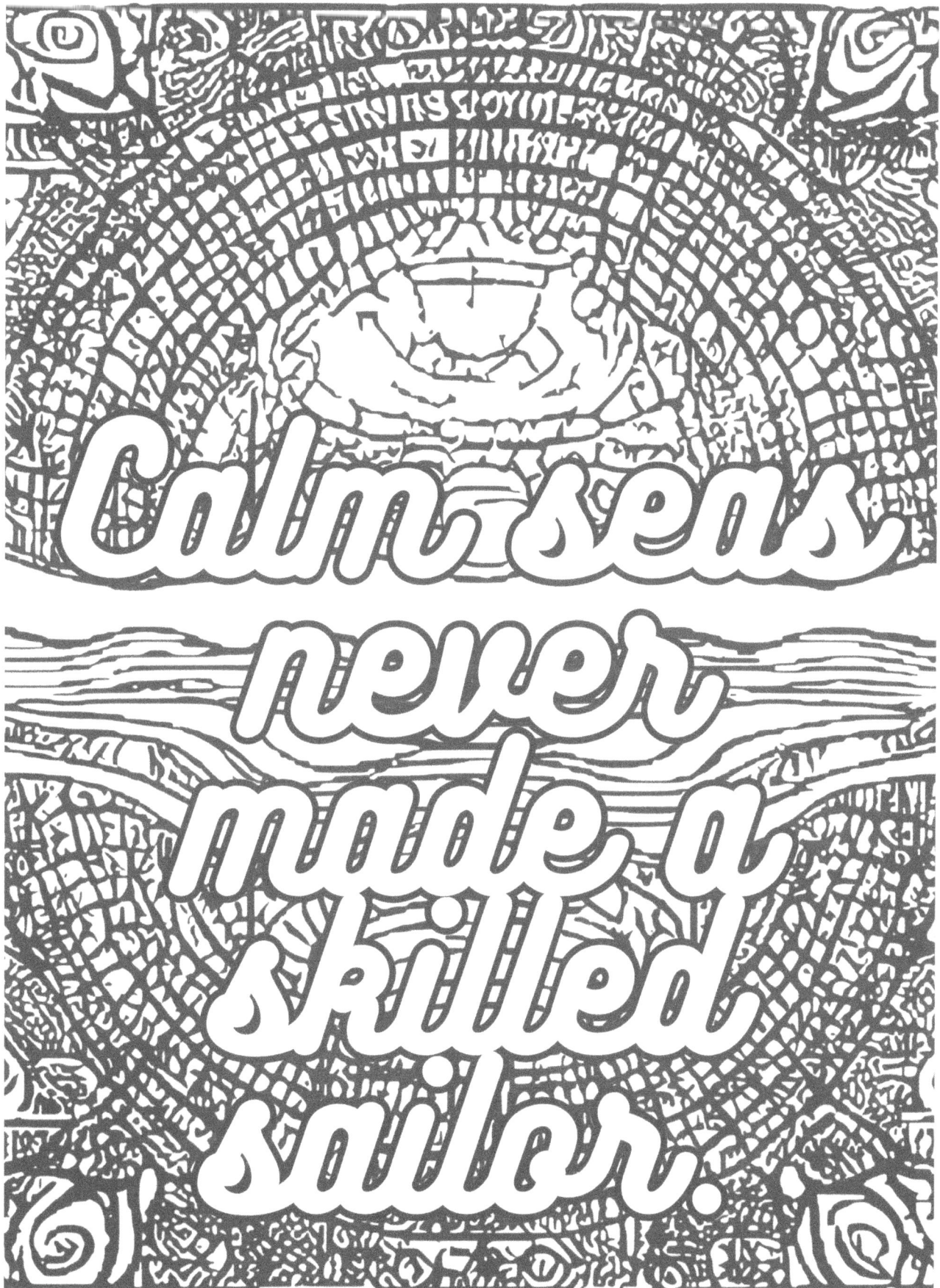

Calm seas never made a skilled sailor.

Difficult roads often lead to beautiful destinations

Believe in yourself you can handle anything

You are Strong and Capable

Life is a journey, find joy in the ride.

Today's challenges are tomorrow's successes

Stress is a reminder to slow down and breathe

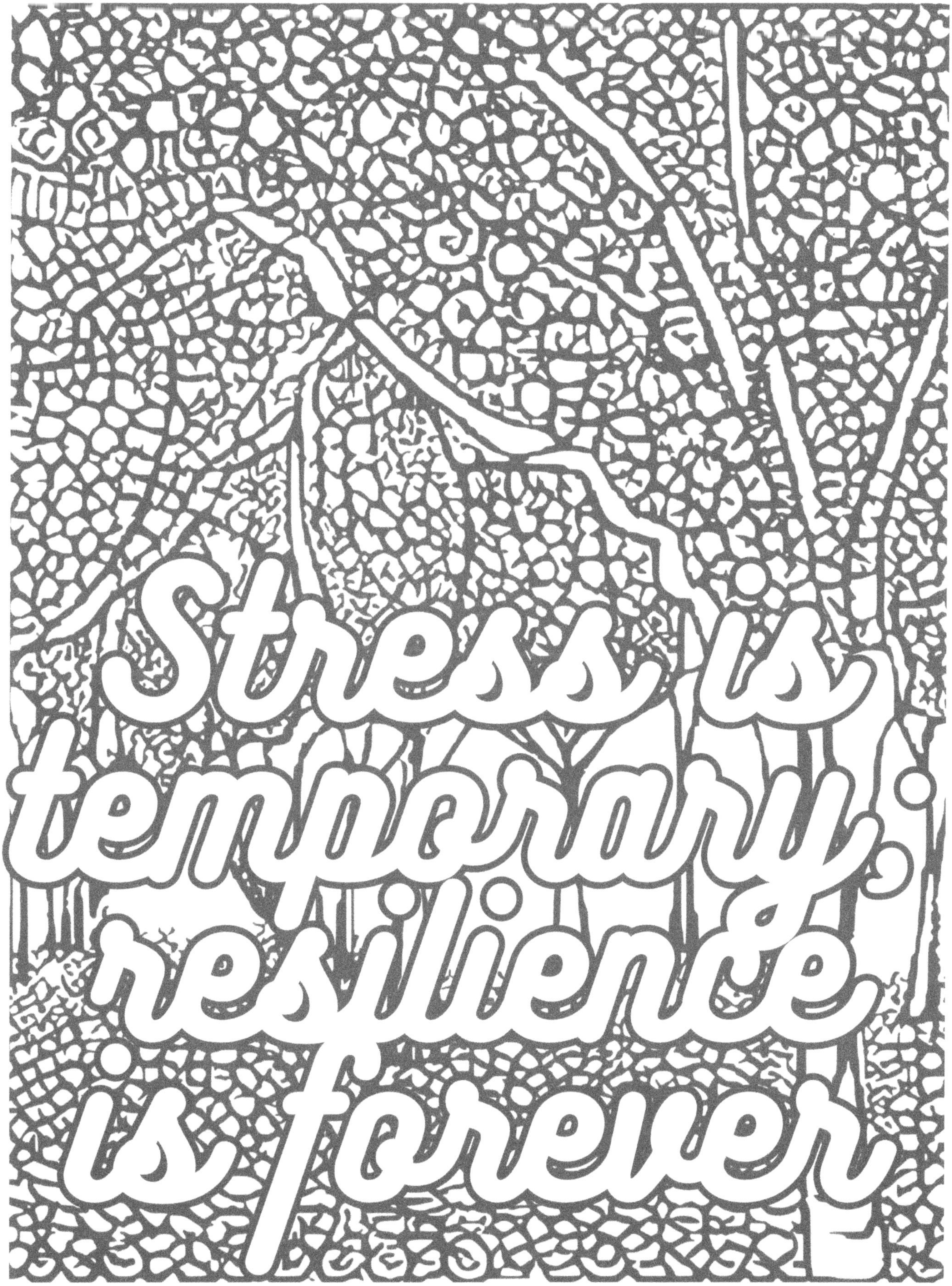
Stress is
temporary,
resilience
is forever

See the positivity in all sitations

Be kind to someone today!

Show Gratitude at all times

Money can't buy Joy

Tomorrow is not Guaranteed to anyone

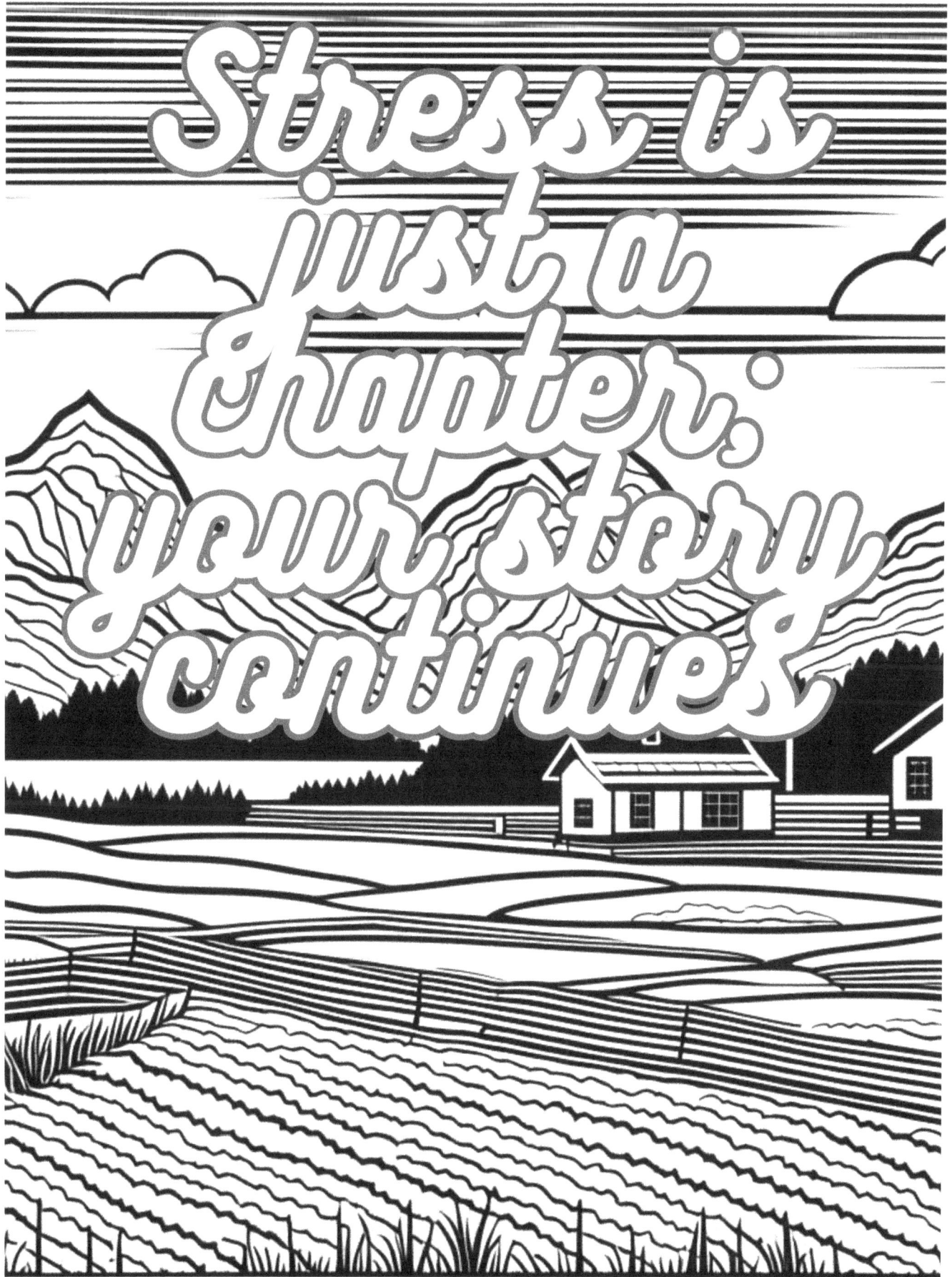

Stress is just a chapter; your story continues

Challenges are an opportunity to grow.

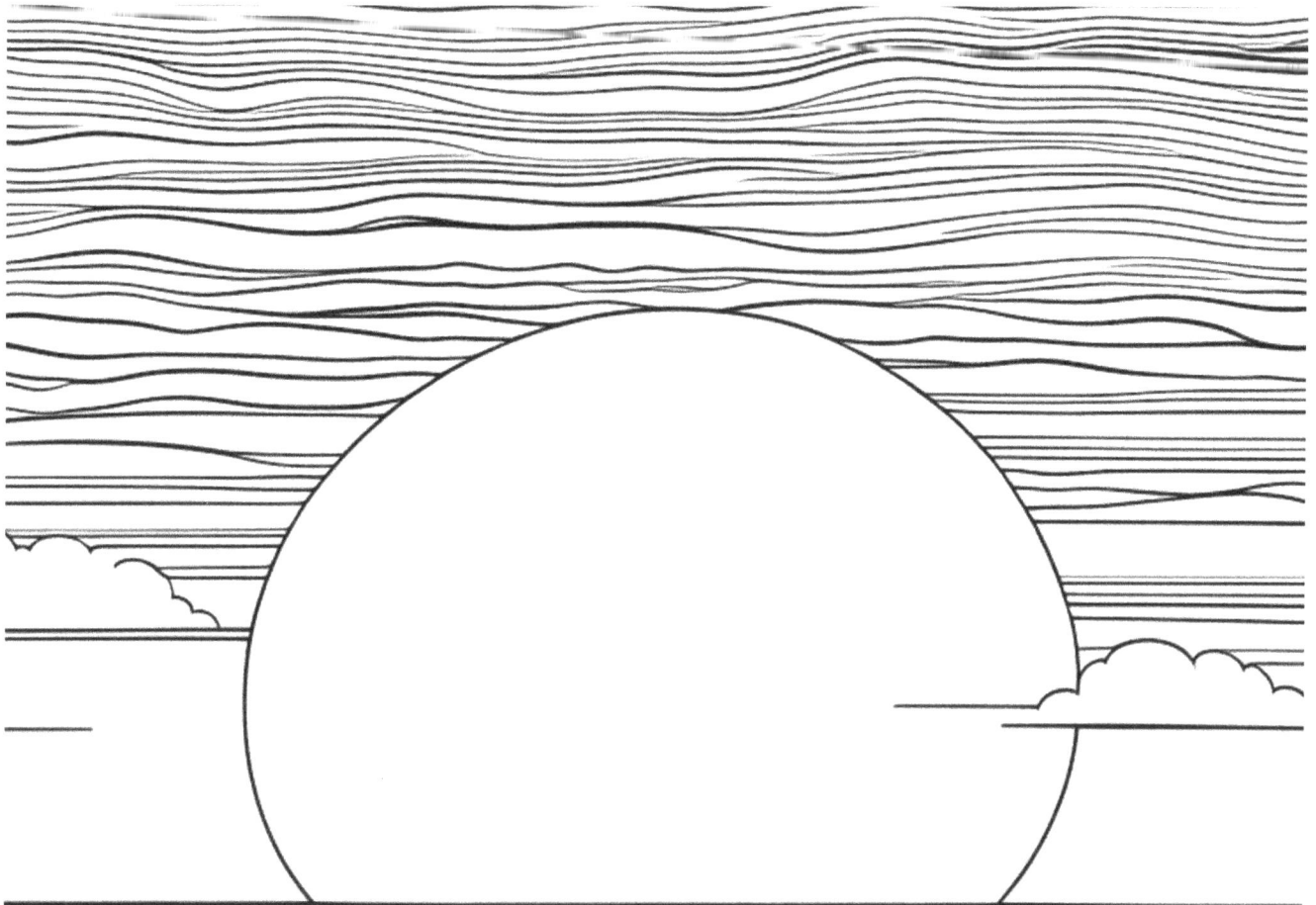

All things are Possible

Obstacles can become opportunitie

Don't give up on your Dreams

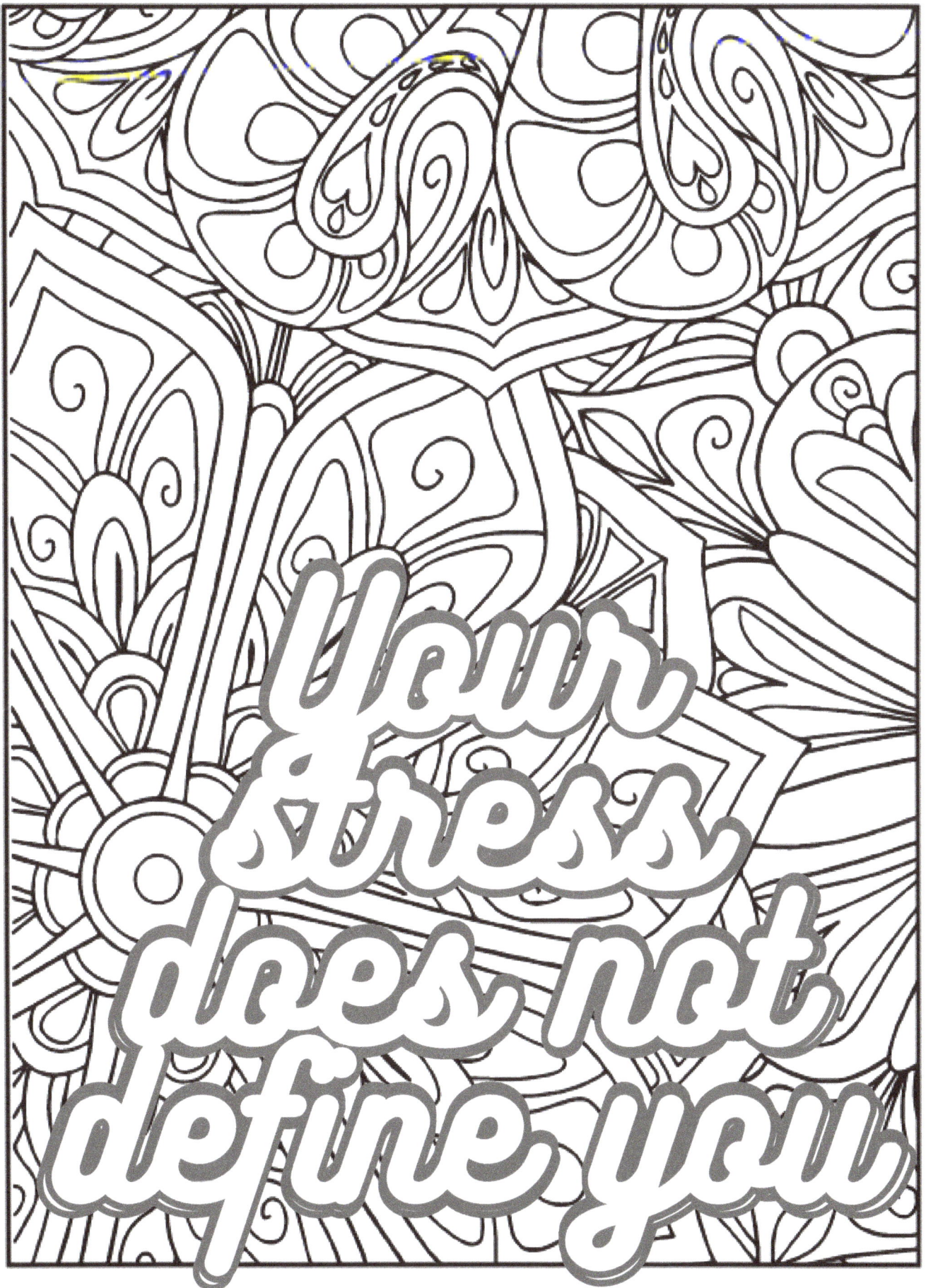

Your Stress does not define you

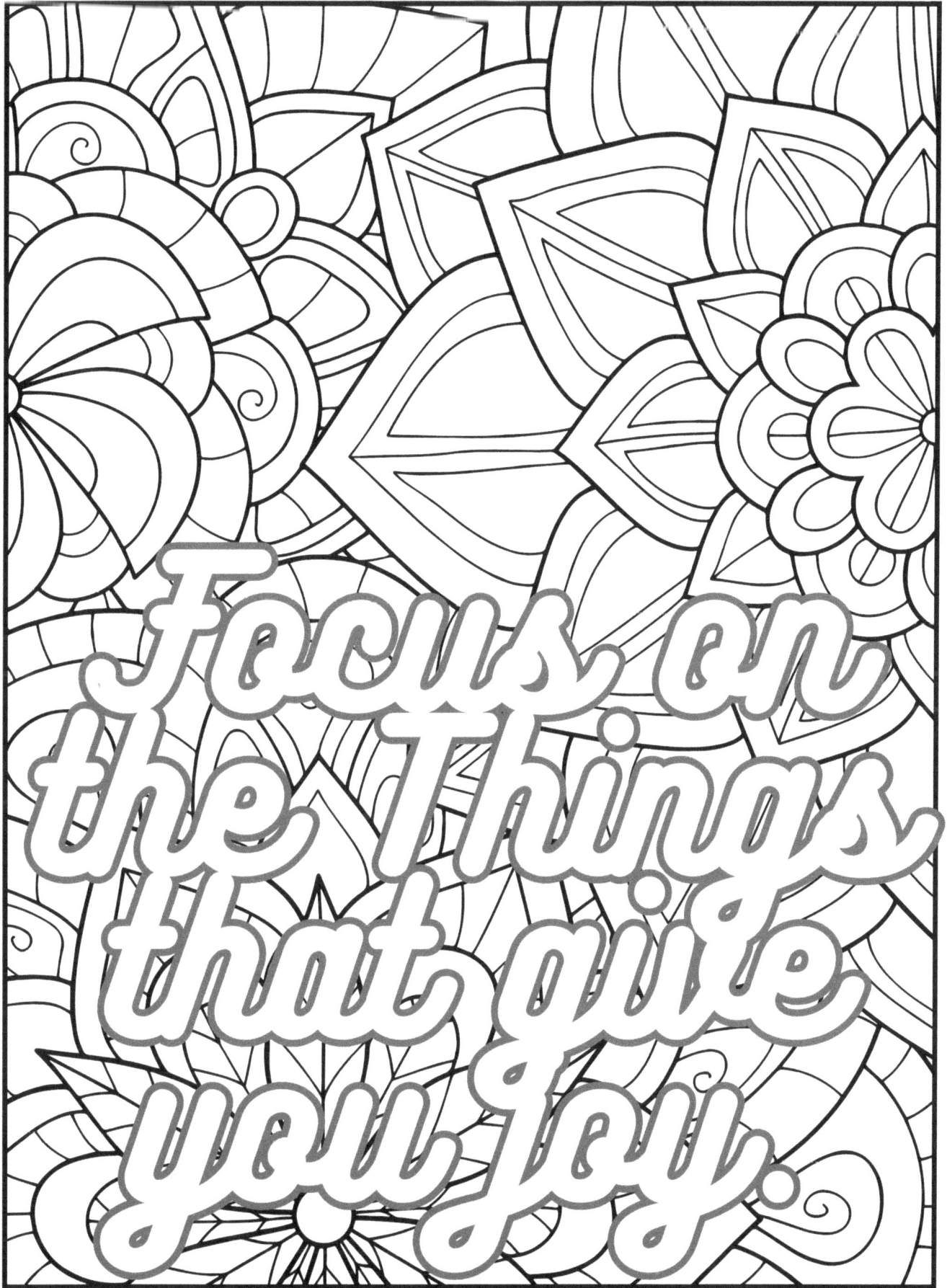

Focus on the Things that give you Joy.

Trust Your Heart

don't stress the loss cherish the gain.

Don't let Stress Rule.

Check out my other books by
Scanning the QR code or using
the link below

linktr.ee/beautyinbooks3

www.ingramcontent.com/pod-product-compliance
Lightning Source LLC
Chambersburg PA
CBHW042346030426
42335CB00031B/3481